# Beasts

© Aladdin Books Ltd 1997

*Designed and produced by*
**Aladdin Books Ltd**
28 Percy Street
London W1P 0LD

ISBN 0 7496 2671 2

*First published in*
*Great Britain in 1997 by*
**Aladdin Books/Watts Books**
96 Leonard Street
London EC2A 4RH

*Editor*
Jim Pipe

*Design*

**David West** • CHILDREN'S BOOKS
*Designer*
Flick Killerby
*Picture Research*
Brooks Krikler Research
*Illustrators*
Francis Phillipps

Printed in Belgium

# FACT *or* FICTION:

# Beasts

Written by *Stewart Ross*
Illustrated by *Francis Phillipps*

**ALADDIN/WATTS**
LONDON · SYDNEY

# Contents

# INTRODUCTION

Human beings live in peace with most creatures. We get on with our business, they get on with theirs. With some species, we have a close working relationship. These are animals like goats, dogs, horses and chickens that, throughout history, have provided us with food, service and friendship.

With certain creatures, however, our relationship is anything but close. These are the beasts! Some are huge and monstrously strong; others lurk in dark corners waiting to strike with their poisonous fangs. There are beasts of the air, forest, mountain and plain. Over the centuries, all have bitten, crushed, poisoned or clawed their terrifying way into our imagination and nightmares.

Beasts have left their mark on all peoples. Aware of their own weakness, humans have feared, respected, even worshipped them for their majesty and power. We have named people after beasts and beasts after people. We have fantasised about them, too, dreaming up creatures even more weird and dreadful than those that actually exist. Enter the dragons, vampires, werewolves and aliens.

So welcome to the safari! Enjoy it and learn from it. But take care – you never know what may be lurking over the next page!

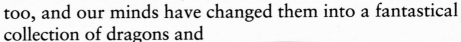

# THE WORLD OF THE BEAST

We have an awesome fascination for beasts. Their power to terrify is far greater than the danger they pose. Fierce tigers, slippery snakes, ravenous wolves (*below*) and poisonous spiders fill us with horror.

We also have a strange respect for beasts, however. Great leaders are often known as the "lion" of their people. Bears and spiders were once worshipped. The snake is as much admired as hated. Hundreds of myths have grown up around such creatures, too, and our minds have changed them into a fantastical collection of dragons and monsters.

**Tiny Terrors**
*Small may be beautiful, but not when it has the power to kill. Of all the dangerous beasts on the planet, perhaps the most feared are those that slither and crawl* (above): *the hooded cobra, erect and ready to strike, the deadly black widow spider or the armoured scorpion.*

### BIG, BEEFY AND BAD
We have always admired the great beasts. Beside the mighty elephant or rhino, our strength is puny. The great cats beat us for speed. Who can match the muscle of the grizzly (*left*), the aggression of the polar bear, or the stealth of the leopard?

And what are our giants compared with those extinct monsters, the dinosaurs, or the huge sabre-toothed tigers (*right*) that must have terrified early humans 20,000 years ago?

## SWOOPING DEATH

Human beings have always wanted to copy the creatures of the air. We first learned to lumber into the air in noisy, awkward machines.

Though today's jets fly so much faster than birds, we still gaze in wonder at the grace and agility of the swooping bird of prey, or marvel at the ability of bats (*right*) and owls to hunt their prey in darkness.

BEASTS AT THE MOVIES. There seems no end to the terrifying monsters that appear on the cinema screen. What lurks in the shadows? A man or a wolf – or some horrifying mix of the two? What creature has left gigantic footprints in the snows of the Himalayas? There must be alien life on another planet. But when will we find it? Or should we worry about little home-grown monsters like the Gremlins (*left*)?

### Horny Beast

*We are by no means the perfect species. In the animal world there are creatures more majestic, more stealthy, more cunning than ourselves.*

*Therefore, all cultures have dreamed up super-beasts that are part-human and part-animal, like the ancient Greek centaur* (right) *that appears in the film* Sinbad and the Eye of the Tiger (1977).

# THE KING OF BEASTS

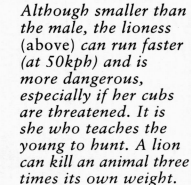

The year was 1900. The plan was to build a 1,300-km railway from Kampala, capital of Uganda, to the port of Mombasa on the Indian Ocean. It was a massive task, but the engineers said it could be done. Building the track soon proved the least of their worries.

At Tsavo, near the foothills of Mount Kilimanjaro, the line had to cross lion territory. The beasts objected. The man-eaters of the Tsavo killed 28 railway workers and work stopped for weeks (*main picture*). Finally, the lions were hunted down and shot. But the local people knew exactly what had been happening: an ancient king and queen had returned as lions to defend their territory.

***Beware the Lioness***
*Although smaller than the male, the lioness (above) can run faster (at 50kph) and is more dangerous, especially if her cubs are threatened. It is she who teaches the young to hunt. A lion can kill an animal three times its own weight.*

## MOTHER'S PRIDE
The largest of the cat family, a lion can weigh over 250 kg and measure 3 m from nose to tail.

Once found from Greece to India, most lions now live in east and southern Africa, usually in family groups (called prides) of one or more adult males and several females.

Using their sharp claws and teeth (*left*), lions will eat almost any creature, from giraffes and 4,000-kg hippopotami to grass mice and tortoises.

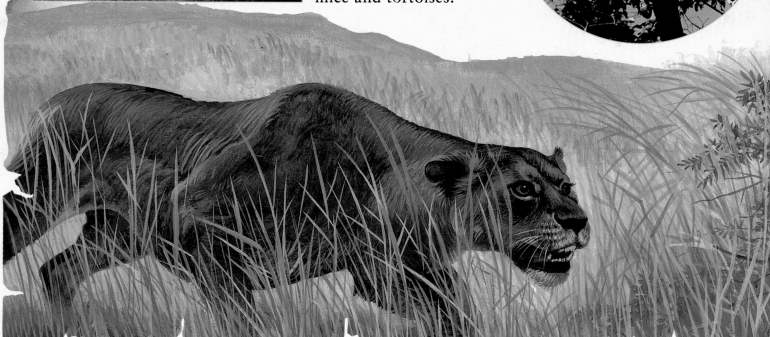

# KING OF BEASTS.

The lion, widely regarded as the king of beasts, is often seen as the symbol of might and power. It is celebrated by the Bapende people of Kongo (*left*), it is the destroyer of demons in Hinduism, the defender of the law in Buddhism and features in many coats of arms, particularly that of British kings and queens.

## Sacred Cats

*To the people of south and central America the jaguar is the master of animals. Mayan rulers were said to be descended from jaguars, and the elite Aztec jaguar warriors dressed like these big cats (above right). Today the jaguar symbol is used by a car manufacturer (right).*

*African priests wear leopard skins. People who believe the leopard is holy may not eat its flesh, since it helps the spirits of the dead.*

## Spot the Leopard?

*Though the leopard (left) weighs just 70 kg, it is a far more cunning predator than the lion. It hunts alone at night, and has been known to drag away human victims without waking up other people living in the same house.*

## TEAM HUNTERS

Healthy lions feed off grazing animals, such as gazelles. They hunt together, stalking their prey downwind and striking with sudden speed and ferocity. But even when lions work in packs, only one in five hunting trips ends in a kill.

Lions' eyes are designed for seeing at night, and most hunts occur just after dark or before sunrise. Older beasts, with failing teeth and strength, may acquire a taste for human flesh, but attacks on people are not common.

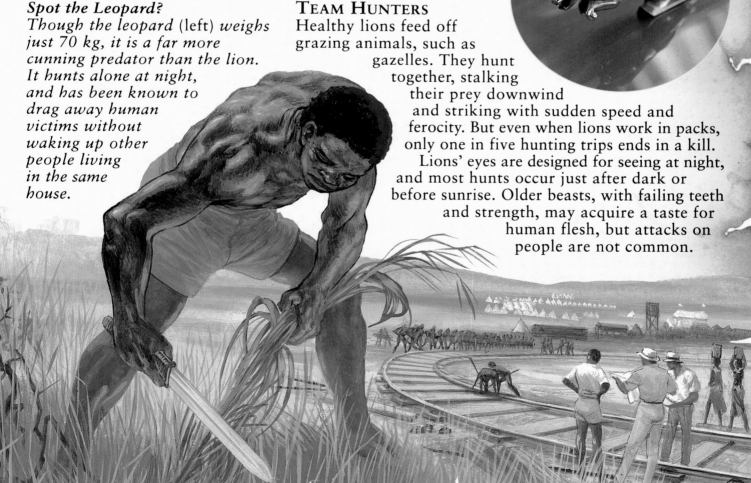

# TIGER TERROR

Bengal, India, 1933. The tiger hunters were perched on top of swaying elephants, heavy rifles at the ready. Ahead of them, beaters worked their way through the undergrowth, shouting and banging drums to drive the tiger into the open. Suddenly, a fearful scream tore the air. A beast had sprung at a young beater from behind, knocking him to the ground.

It seized him in its powerful jaws and began dragging him into the bushes. The other beaters ran to help him. The tiger lifted its bloody head, paused a second (*right*), then left its prey and sloped off into the jungle.

**EASY, TIGER!** (*above* and *top*)
The graceful tiger, which grows to about the same size as a lion, once roamed widely over much of Asia. Although normally marked with distinctive stripes, cream or black tigers have been known.

When injured, threatened or unable to find deer or game, tigers may become human-eaters. They are also strong swimmers, unlike most cats, and can adapt to habitats ranging from icy mountains to tropical jungles.

*The Fisher Cat*
*The jaguar* (left) *is the New World's biggest cat. A skillful fisher, it scoops fish from the water with its paws.*

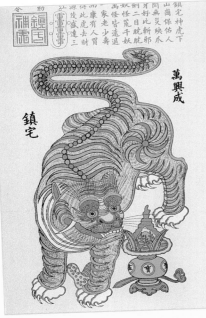

## SACRED STRIPES

In Eastern mythology, the tiger is the lord of the land animals (*left*). It is a symbol of power and royalty, and even today parts of a tiger's body are highly prized for their strength-giving properties. The Rajputs, Indian princes, claim to be descended from tigers, and Hindu gods are shown riding tigers or dressed in their skins.

THE WERETIGER. In Malaysia, the tiger was known as "whisker face" or the "stripy one". To mention it by name risked calling up the weretiger. These were the souls of the dead, in human form, that could change into vicious tigers (*right*). The Javanese also had weretigers, but happily they used their powers for good rather than evil.

### Tigger not Tiger
*A.A. Milne's Tigger is the world's most un-beastly tiger. When he first bounces up at Winnie-the-Pooh's house (in the middle of the night), he attacks the table cloth because he thinks it is trying to bite him. In spite of his boasting, Tigger is loved by everyone – except when he gets too bouncy!*

SHEER MAJESTY. Sheer Khan (meaning the "prince without guilt"), the famous fictional tiger of Rudyard Kipling's *Jungle Book* (1894), was a majestic figure feared by all the creatures of the jungle (*above*, face-to-face with Mowgli in the 1993 film).

### Beastly Sprinter
*Lithe and muscular, the cheetah (right) is the fastest of all land animals. It uses speed rather than stealth to catch its prey (antelopes and smaller mammals) and, in short bursts, can run at an amazing 110 kph!*

# MAD ELEPHANT!

In the 1920s, English writer George Orwell worked as a policeman in Burma. One day, an elephant went berserk (*main picture*), smashing a house, killing a cow and crushing a van. It then stamped on a man. The animal's weight pushed the poor fellow 30 cm into the mud.

Orwell borrowed a gun and, watched by a huge crowd, killed the creature. What had happened? Elephants are sensitive animals that can be angered by being badly treated. Once a year, male elephants also go through *must*, a period when increased hormone levels can make them very aggressive.

## BIG EARS

Elephants are distinguished by size (the larger African, *top*, is up to 3.5 m tall and can weigh a massive 6 tonnes), shape (the Indian's head is concave, the African's convex) and ear-size (the African's ears are larger).

The African elephant is more aggressive than its Indian cousin, but both are intelligent – and they really do have good memories! Mammoths (*right*) – the elephant's 10,000 year-old ancestors – had tusks 4 m long. During the great Ice Age, many grew long hair on their bodies.

### Angry and Ancient

*The weak-eyed rhino* (left), *the second largest land beast, is a 2-tonne mammal that has been around in one form or another for 40 million years.*

*Sporting either one (if Indian) or two (if African) horns, this short-tempered living tank will charge humans at great speed – not to eat them (it feeds on leaves) but to drive them away.*

## HUNTING HORNS

Rhino horns are made of compressed bristles and are not attached to the skull. Unfortunately, as their horns are a prized ingredient in Oriental medicine, rhinos have been hunted almost to extinction.

## WORKING ANIMALS

The creature in George Orwell's *Shooting An Elephant* was a working elephant. The Indian elephant, which is usually not aggressive and can be easily trained, has long been used in building, agriculture and war.

There is still a force of over 5,000 trained elephants working in the timber industry in Myanmar (formerly Burma).

***Stampede!***
*In the film Jumanji (1995), a magical game unleashes a herd of African animals onto a small town in the United States (left), with terrifying results.*

*This image of mad stampeding animals is very different to traditional African myth, where the elephant is portrayed as being too noble for its own good.*

HOLY HERDS. People have always thought the elephant intelligent. The Greek philosopher Aristotle reckoned it was the brainiest beast, while Roman writer Pliny said elephants worshipped the sun. Hindus show Ganesha, god of wisdom, with an elephant's head (*right*), and use real elephants in their ceremonies (*top*).

Rare white elephants do exist. A King of Thailand gave them to courtiers he wanted to get rid of. From this we get the term, "white elephant", meaning useless or bound to fail.

# A REAL DRAGON

In 1983, on the Indonesian island of Komodo, a mother left her small boy for a few minutes while she went to visit her sick aunt. Before she left, she warned the child not to go too near the edge of the forest, but the boy was soon chasing bright-coloured bugs into the bushes. There was a rustling in the undergrowth. Before the child had time to scream, a huge Komodo dragon was upon him (*main picture*). The vicious Komodo has been known to grow up to 3 m in length and 166 kg in weight. Swift and powerful, it has been blamed for 26 human deaths in the last 65 years.

### Lounging Lizard
*Though they can look pretty disgusting to humans, most lizards are shy, harmless creatures. The marine iguana* (above), *for example, is 1.8 m long, but can't even eat plants – it mostly feeds on tiny algae in the sea.*

## A LITTLE SQUIRT
There are some horrible beasts among the 3,000 lizard species. The bright-orange gila monster (or beaded lizard, *bottom*) of North and Central America is poisonous, but because its venom works slowly, it has to hang onto a victim with its vice-like jaws.

The horned toad drives off intruders by squirting a jet of blood from the corner of each eye. But most lizards try to avoid other animals. They use tricks like hissing and swelling up to appear fiercer than they really are.

S HINE KNIGHT. The most famous dragon-slayer is St. George, patron saint of England and Portugal. The real St. George was killed by the Romans in 303 AD for being a Christian. The hero of myth (*left*) was a knight in shining armour who saved a fair maiden by slaying a terrible dragon.

### Shake the Lizard
*Another big lizard is the Nile monitor of Africa, which grows to about 2 m. It digs, runs and swims well and can climb trees. Like many lizard species, the monitor is a big flesh-eater. So watch out for your fingers!*

**D**RAGONS NEVER DIE. Our fascination with dragons never dies. Fire-breathing flappers, such as Smaug (the evil dragon in J.R.R. Tolkien's *The Hobbit*, 1937), have become popular figures in children's literature.

The film *Dragonheart* (1996, *right*) carried on the tradition with its talking dragon, Draco.

### Friend or Foe?

*Hindu and Christian dragons were evil beasts, representing chaos or the devil. The Chinese dragon was a symbol of the emperor's power, or luck (the lucky dragon on the right is at a New Year celebration). The Celts had dragons as war symbols on their banners.*

**S**LIPPERY GUARD. *The ancient Greeks saw the dragon, a flying crocodile with a long tail, as a guardian of precious things. In fact, the word "dragon" comes from the Greek drakon, meaning "to see".*

*Greek myths are full of dragon stories. For his eleventh labour, Hercules had to steal three golden apples from the Garden of Hesperides at the edge of the world. But he had to sneak past the guardian dragon first (left).*

# BATTLE OF THE DINOS

It looks no contest. The multi-tonne Iguanodon is many times the size of the attacking Deinonychus. One blow from its massive tail could smash their bones like sticks. But the Deinonychus, ruthless pack hunters, are more intelligent and nimble than their lumbering prey. Within minutes the Iguanodon, its flesh ripped with gaping wounds, crashes to the ground and the attackers move in for the kill.

There were dozens of different types of dinosaur. Most, like the Iguanodon or the huge Ultrasaurus (*bottom*), were plant eaters (or herbivores), unlike the meat-eating (or carnivorous) Deinonychus.

***Beastly Imagination*** (main picture)
*All pictures of dinosaurs are partly based on guesswork. But though they ruled the Earth between about 225 and 65 million years ago, studies of fossils have taught us a lot about how dinosaurs looked.*

***Deinonychus*** *means "terrible claw", after the razor-sharp talon (above) on one toe from each foot that was designed to flick forward and slash its prey.*

## WHAT HAPPENED?
Today's fossil experts (called palaeontologists) are confused by one great mystery – why did dinosaurs become extinct? Many theories have been suggested, but the most likely is that they could not survive the cold weather that followed after a meteor hit the Earth.

***Dragon Bones***
*Many ancient Chinese medicine recipes contained "dragon bones" – but these were in fact dinosaur fossils!*

## KING OF THE KILLERS
*Tyrannosaurus rex* was the one of the largest flesh-eating beasts ever. It stood 7 m high, measured 15 m from nose to tail and weighed about 7 tonnes. It could run at 50 kph, but only in short bursts, so it often ambushed prey.

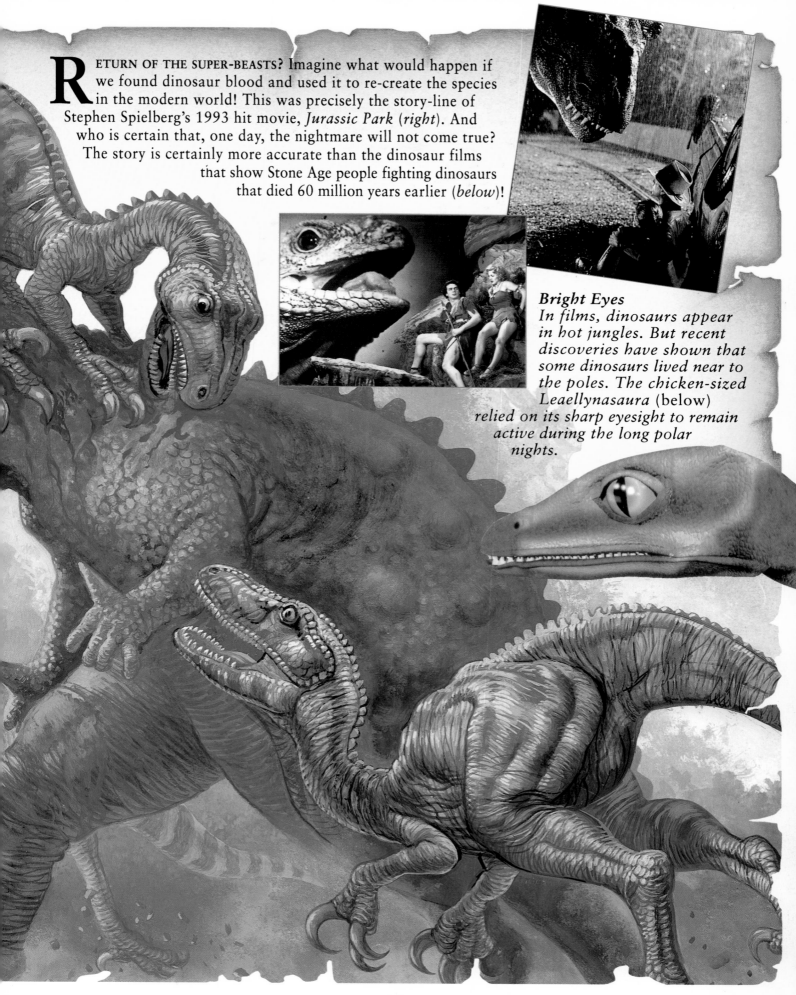

RETURN OF THE SUPER-BEASTS? Imagine what would happen if we found dinosaur blood and used it to re-create the species in the modern world! This was precisely the story-line of Stephen Spielberg's 1993 hit movie, *Jurassic Park* (*right*). And who is certain that, one day, the nightmare will not come true? The story is certainly more accurate than the dinosaur films that show Stone Age people fighting dinosaurs that died 60 million years earlier (*below*)!

**Bright Eyes**
In films, dinosaurs appear in hot jungles. But recent discoveries have shown that some dinosaurs lived near to the poles. The chicken-sized Leaellynasaura (*below*) relied on its sharp eyesight to remain active during the long polar nights.

# CUDDLY KILLERS

In the still of the early morning, a group of Inuit hunters in northern Canada heard a scuffling noise outside their tent. Suspecting a thief, one of the men went to investigate. It was indeed a thief – not a human one, but a massive polar bear! Terrified, the hunter edged towards the tent.

The great white beast followed, rearing up on its hind legs (*main picture*). Seconds later, a blow from the bear's powerful paw snapped his neck. Polar bears, the world's largest carnivores, are said to be the only bears that deliberately hunt humans for food. One explanation is that the weak-eyed creatures mistake Inuits dressed in seal-skin clothing for their favourite food – seals!

### Grizzly Swipes
*The grizzly bear (Ursus horribilis, below right) is a more aggressive cousin of the brown bear. It does not hug its enemies to death, as once believed, but swipes at them with deadly 14-cm claws. Despite being 2 m tall and weighing 500 kg, it can run faster than an Olympic sprinter!*

### UN–BEAR–ABLE?

The intelligent brown bear (*above*) was once common in many parts of Europe. It is now found in north and central Asia and North America. In colder habitats, the beasts hibernate during the winter.

Bears generally prefer to avoid people. Although vicious if threatened (especially if guarding cubs), the brown bear is not normally dangerous. But stay clear of the Asian black bear – although small, it is unpredictably vicious!

Brown Bear

Black Bear

### Big Drifters
*Polar bears, distinguished by their white fur, long necks and small heads, inhabit the Arctic ice cap, Greenland, Canada and Russia.*

*Drifting on ice floes, they have travelled as far south as Iceland. Thick fur (which covers the pads of the feet to help grip the ice) and layers of fat enable them to survive the freezing conditions. They supplement their usual diet of fish and seals (and the occasional person!) with berries and grass.*

## FURRY ANCESTORS

Humans have always thought that bears were rather special creatures. This has not always been to their advantage: prehistoric peoples sacrificed them to the gods. Celtic goddesses, such as Artio (*left*), were also shown as bears, while early Christians thought bears carried the devil (*right*)! Some primitive peoples believed humans were descended from a bear, the "Animal Master".

### Hey, Good Licking!

*The saying "licked into shape" comes from the belief that this is what mother bears did to their cubs, which were born without shape! "Teddy" bears are named after big game hunting US president Teddy Roosevelt, who in 1902 refused to shoot a bear cub.*

## STARRY BEARS

In Greek myth, bears were sacred to Artemis, goddess of hunting. When the nymph Callisto had a son by the god Zeus, his jealous wife changed her into a bear. The nymph and her son eventually became stars – the Great (*above*) and Little Bear constellations are still named after them.

THOR'S BEARS. In Northern Europe the bear, rather than the lion, was the king of animals. The Viking god Thor (*right*) kept two bears: Alta (the mother of all things female) and Alti (the father of all things male).

# THE ABOMINABLE SNOWMAN

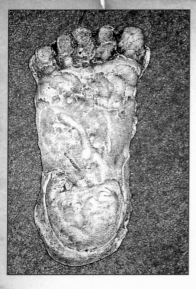

In 1951, British explorer Eric Shipton returned from the Himalayas with photographs of strange footprints. The locals had told him they were the tracks of the "Abominable Snowman", or Yeti. Three years later Ralph Izzard and Tom Stobbart set out to discover the truth. In the mountains they too came across tracks in the snow (*main picture*), but no beast.

Later, an excited yak-herder said he had heard a Yeti calling in the night. After passing on the news, he went straight to the monastery to be purified – for local people believe that bad luck falls on all who hear the cry of the Yeti.

**Fearsome Footprints**
*According to Tom Stobbart, the four-toed Yeti footprints seen in 1954 measured 32 cm by 20 cm. This compares with the cast of American Yeti, Big Foot (above left), taken in 1990 in Washington State, which measured 36 cm by 17.5 cm. Most reports say the Yeti is about 3 m tall and weighs 140 kg.*

## FALSE FIENDS?
Nothing grabs the headlines quite like a monster sighting, and it takes only a suitably blurry photograph and a vivid imagination. Hoaxers have dressed in bear skins, laid false footprints and even made false animal dung! Either of the Bigfoot pictures *above* could have been faked – but only the photographers know the truth.

**T**HE ABOMINABLE BUDDY. Not all strange beasts are abominable (meaning disgusting)! In the film the *Abominable Snowman* (1957) the yeti was hunted by cruel humans. The gentle giant later starred in the film *Big Foot and the Hendersons* (1987, *below*) in which it was adopted by a loving family.

## STRANGE CREATURES

The Yeti (*right*) is known as Meti, Shookpa or Kang-Min, depending on which part of Asia it is seen in, and Bigfoot or Sasquatch in America. Another mysterious animal is the Gulo. In Swedish myth, this monster only died when it burst its stomach trying to squeeze between two trees in search of food. Its hooves were supposed to provide a cure for earache! The Gulo may be based on the wolverine, a bear-like mammal with a huge appetite.

**radar**

**I**NNER BEAUTY? Among the many tales of humans being turned into beasts, *Beauty and the Beast* is one of the most popular (*left*). The story makes the point that not everything that looks ugly on the outside is always beastly by nature.

# THE BIG BAD WOLF

*What Big Teeth You Have*
*The wolf's jaw (below)* can *exert a pressure of 105 kg/cm², twice that of an Alsatian dog.*

The wolf, once common in most of Asia and Europe, is now returning to many of its old hunting grounds. It is a hunter and scavenger that sometimes operates in huge packs. Although its normal diet is small wild mammals, it has a fearful reputation because starving packs have attacked children or weakened adults. Russian wolf packs were said to have pursued sleighs to get at their terrified passengers. The grey wolf, "prairie wolf" (coyote) and Arctic wolf (*top*) were less dangerous.

## HOWLING AND LAUGHING

There is no sound more certain to send a shiver down the spine than the howl of the wolf (*above*). But the wolf howl is not a signal to attack, any more than a hyena's "laugh" (*left*) means that it is enjoying itself. Wolves howl for many reasons, such as making contact, calling a pack meeting, or just out of loneliness. A howl lasts up to 20 seconds and each wolf has its own "voice".

*Wolf Expressions – like humans, wolves use their faces to show how they're feeling: 1 = angry, 2 = aggressive, 3 = afraid and 4 = terrified.*

## A BAD REPUTATION

The view of the wolf as a cold-blooded human killer dates from the 14th century, when the Black Death killed a third of people in Europe. Wolves were very common and probably scavenged the remains of the dead. Medieval tales like Little Red Riding Hood (*above*) spread the message: "Don't trust a wolf"!

In fact, wolf attacks on humans are very rare. Wolves will even eat worms, insects and berries when meat is scarce.

**B**EWARE THE FULL MOON. The myth of the werewolf was once widespread in Europe – and is still popular at the movies (such as this beast from *An American Werewolf in London*, 1983, *above*). The werewolf is a human who changes into a wolf, usually during full moon.

*Native Americans greatly respected the wolf, which was often seen as a cultural hero and the remote ancestor by some tribes. Its symbol was the Dog Star, said to be the home of the gods.*

### CALL OF NATURE

American novelist Jack London (1876–1916) wrote many of the finest tales of the frozen world of the husky dog and the wolf.

The best-known are *White Fang* and *The Call of the Wild*, made into a film in 1972 (*left*).

# THE HOUND FROM HELL

The mist lay thick and damp over the gloomy moor. Crouched beside the path, Sherlock Holmes, Lestrade and Dr Watson heard a swift pattering sound. Holmes cocked his gun. Then, the hound was upon them. Lestrade collapsed with a cry of horror. Even Holmes was paralysed by the hellish sight.

Then, raising his revolver, he fired. Watson fired too and the pair set off in pursuit. They arrived to see the monster leap at Sir Henry Baskerville's throat, throwing him to the ground (*main picture*). An instant later Holmes emptied his gun into the beast's side – and the Hound of the Baskervilles was dead.

*Horrible Hounds*
*The legendary Hound of the Baskervilles was a hound-mastiff cross. Most real dogs are very friendly, but the vicious pitbull terrier* (below) *has been known to attack for no obvious reason.*

## WILD RELATIVES

The dog family has many small but wild relatives. Among the best-known are the scavenging jackal (*below*), the Australian dingo and the fox. None of these species is a real danger to humans.

Big-biting hyenas, which feed off the left-overs of other carnivores, are said in African folklore to carry witches at night!

## THE SURVIVORS

Foxes (*below*) are one of Nature's great survivors. As their rural habitat has shrunk, many have moved to the towns, where they survive on garbage.

### The Wily Fox

*People have a strange love-hate relationship with the cunning fox. The English hunt it on horseback during the day then return home in the evening to read jolly stories about it to their children. The African-American character Brer Fox (top) is part of an African tradition of clever foxes that also appears in Aesop's Fables.*

## SOUL SHEPHERD.

The ancient Egyptian god Anubis had a human body topped off with a jackal's head (*left*). He took control of the souls of the dead when they entered hell and herded them before the Great Judge to be told their fate.

### Once Bitten, Twice Shy

*Infection with disease rabies after a dog or fox bite is far worse than the wound itself (right). Luckily, powerful drugs are now available to cure infected humans.*

# MONKEY BUSINESS

The earliest written reports said the gorilla was a ferocious beast. It was reported to kill people and even attack elephants that disturbed it. The friendly looking chimpanzee, on the other hand, was popular from the start. The first specimen to reach London zoo travelled by coach, sitting inside beside its keeper! Rarely have we been more deceived by appearances.

The gorilla is a peaceful creature that lives on plants, while the chimp is one of the world's most aggressive animals. Chimps roam through the forest, leaving a trail of destruction. And it is not just the vegetation that suffers. Gangs of chimps actively hunt down monkeys and even other chimps using ruthless tactics that give their prey no chance of escape.

*Monkey Spite*
*A baby baboon that has lost its way is viciously attacked by a troop of aggressive chimpanzees (right).*

### ALL IN THE FAMILY
Humans are members of the primate family, which includes bushbabies and lemurs. Apes (gibbons, chimps, gorillas and orangutans) are our nearest relatives.

Monkeys are distant, largely tree-dwelling cousins, though baboons (*top* and *right*) spend much of their time on the ground. Several African and Asian varieties have spectacularly unattractive bottoms. Many American species have tails that can grasp objects like a hand.

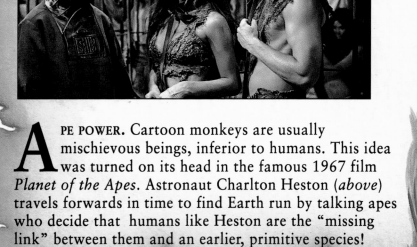

**A**PE POWER. Cartoon monkeys are usually mischievous beings, inferior to humans. This idea was turned on its head in the famous 1967 film *Planet of the Apes*. Astronaut Charlton Heston (*above*) travels forwards in time to find Earth run by talking apes who decide that humans like Heston are the "missing link" between them and an earlier, primitive species!

**Idols or Idiots?**
*The ancient Chinese considered the monkey to be one of the Three Senseless Creatures. The Hindus of India, on the other hand, thought their monkey god Hanuman was clever, skilful and loyal (right).*

**G**ENTLE GIANTS. Once called "pongos", gorillas are the giants of the ape family. The huge vegetarians, standing almost 2 m tall and weighing 250 kg, are famous for beating their chests. This is a sign of excitement, not anger.

Films like *King Kong* (*below*) made many people think that gorillas were ferocious. But *Gorillas in the Mist* (1988), which told the story of Dianne Fossey's study of mountain gorillas, highlighted their gentle nature.

**Mystic Monkey Trio**
*Mythology's most famous monkeys are the Three Mystic Monkeys of Japan. With paws covering their eyes, ears and mouth, they stand for: "Speak no evil", "See no evil" and "Hear no evil" (below).*

27

# CLAWS FROM THE SKY

In Medieval Europe, it happened every year, as surely as spring followed winter. The eagles came hunting the lambs. Armed only with slings and bows, there was little the shepherds could do to guard their sheep. One minute the flock would be grazing peacefully. The next – a beating of wings, a chorus of terrified bleating – and another lamb was carried off to eager beaks in a distant eyrie (nest).

Eagles are not always as bold and fierce as they look, however. Most will eat the easiest meal available, including carrion (dead animals). They generally avoid humans and will only attack if cornered, especially when defending their nests.

## Snatch!

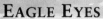

*Daylight hunters – such as falcons (left), buzzards, hawks, merlins and kestrels – circle or hover above their prey, waiting for the chance to strike. Peregrine falcons drop from the sky at incredible speeds (up to 350 kph), snatching their prey with clawed talons.*

## EAGLE EYES

All hunting birds have remarkable hearing and eyesight. The night-hunting owl can detect the scuffling of a mouse many metres away, and its unusual, forward-facing eyes allow it to zero in on its target with deadly precision. A single pair of owls will clear a wide area of thousands of rats and mice.

## KINGS OF THE AIR

Although only a few of the 8,500 species of bird hunt living mammals, the power, speed and grace of these creatures are awesome. The golden eagle, with a 2-m wingspan, is widely seen as the king of birds. Since ancient times, people have trained captive eagles (*left*), hawks and falcons to hunt for them.

**Poised for the Kill**
Until firearms were
used to scare them off,
eagles were a problem
at spring time (below).

**Holy Hawks**
All cultures respected
the swift hawk (right). To
the ancient Greeks and the
Aztecs, it was a messenger
for the gods. Some Native
American peoples believed a hawk
helped to create the world. The Ainu of
Japan sacrificed hawks with the prayer:
"Divine hawk, you are an expert hunter,
let your cleverness fall on me."

## A SIGN OF STRENGTH

Because the mighty
eagle was thought to be
able to fly nearer the
sun than other
creatures, and
even look at it
without blinking, it
became a symbol of
power and victory.
Not surprisingly, many peoples
made it their emblem. Roman
soldiers were prepared to die for their
eagle standards (*left*). Russian and Austrian
emperors also used eagles as their symbols, and the United
States chose the bald eagle as its national bird in 1782.

**P**AINFUL PECKER. According to
Greek legend, Prometheus was
punished by Zeus, king of the
gods, by being chained to a
mountain and having his liver pecked
out by an eagle (*right*). As his
liver grew again during
the night, his horrible ordeal
was repeated day after day!

**The Hunter Hunted**
Today many species of birds of prey,
such as the Java hawk and the
Monkey-eating eagle, are under
threat as their forest homes are
destroyed. Though eagles are
protected in most countries, they
are still hunted illegally for sport.

29

# UGLY VULTURES

The image is universal: a dry, barren landscape; the exhausted traveller, sprawled on the ground, dying slowly of thirst; nearby a flock of hideous vultures, sitting in silence (*left*), watch intently for life to leave the body before they swoop down to feed.

The vulture's reputation is not a pleasant one. No one likes beasts that feed off dead bodies. The bird's bald neck, scraggy plumage and bloody markings make its appearance as repulsive as its eating habits (*main picture*). Yet scavengers are just as important in the food chain as hunters. And though hideous at close quarters, a vulture in flight is a majestic sight.

*Bare-faced Raiders*
*Vultures' heads and necks are bare (above) because any feathers here would get soaked in blood when they feed!*

## CARRION EATING
Vultures (*above*) are the largest scavenger birds. In northern regions dead bodies are cleaned up by members of the crow family, which includes the jet black raven and rook, and the many varieties of gull.

### Thunderbirds are Grow!
*The Thunderbird carved on totem poles (right) was sacred to many Native American peoples — they believed it fertilised the earth.*

*Flying Messengers of Death*
*Odin, the Viking god of the dead, left his dirty work to a dozen or so maidens, the Valkyries. They flew down to a battle on horseback and cut down those selected to go to their master's hall, Valhalla.*

UNINVITED GUESTS. The Harpies (*right*) were hag-faced vultures from Greek mythology that swooped down on feasts, devouring everything. Like most flying things, they were famous for their disgusting droppings!

HORRIBLE HERALD. In mythology, the raven is the messenger of death. It was later immortalised in Edgar Allen Poe's poem, *The Raven*. No one likes scavengers, but the raven's deep rumbling croak, purple-black feathers and fact that it is often seen alone make it appear even more sinister.

*Raven*

DARK DEEDS. The bad reputation of the vulture was used to good effect in the 1982 film, *The Dark Crystal* (*left*), in which a captive planet fights against an evil race of vulture-like aliens who like nothing better than feasting on rotting food!

# BLOODSUCKERS

Shortly after his arrival in Colombia in 1624, Pedro de Alvares joined some Spaniards on a long trip through the jungle. Because of the heat, he slept under a thin sheet. During the third night, a small creature landed silently near where he lay.

It ran swiftly to his bare feet and bit a slice of skin from one of his toes. Pedro stirred as the vampire bat lapped greedily at the flowing blood. In the morning, Pedro noticed the bite mark and the bloodstains, but thought nothing of them. Two days later gangrene set in. The infection spread to his foot, then to his leg. A fortnight later, he was dead.

## NOCTURNAL MISSIONS
Bats (*top*) are not blind. However, to aid night navigation (*below*) they have developed a natural "radar" system.

They send out high-pitched waves of sound that bounce off objects and are then picked up by the bats' sharp ears. Some bats are capable of long journeys at night using natural features, such as river beds, as "roads".

*Dirty Guzzlers* (main picture)
*Although vampire bats take little blood, the wounds they make are dangerous. Victims sometimes die from blood poisoning or infections caught from dirty fangs* (above).

*Vampire fangs*

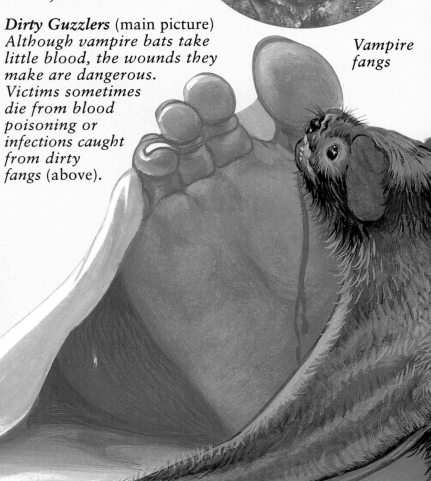

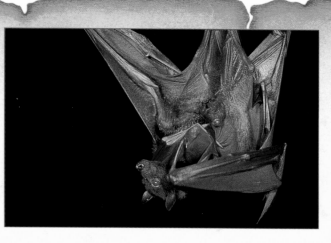

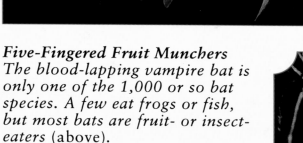

## THEY SUCK!

The true bloodsuckers are not bats but leeches, ticks and insects like mosquitoes (*right*). All are more dangerous for the infections and disease they can cause than the amount of blood they consume.

Tropical leeches were once used by doctors to "bleed" patients and they are still a useful source of *hirudin*, a chemical that keeps the blood flowing.

### Five-Fingered Fruit Munchers
*The blood-lapping vampire bat is only one of the 1,000 or so bat species. A few eat frogs or fish, but most bats are fruit- or insect-eaters (above).*

*All bats are active at night (nocturnal), with wings of skin attached to five-fingered "hands". Wingspans range from 1.5 m for some tropical bats, to about 80 mm for some of their tiny European cousins.*

B RAM'S BEAST. Human vampires return from the grave to drink the blood of the living. In legend, they have the power to turn into bats or mist. Perhaps the most famous vampire story is Bram Stoker's chilling *Dracula* (1897, *below*). The tale of the blood-sucking Transylvanian count, based on the exploits of the real Vlad the Impaler (1456–1476), has spawned hundreds of horror movies, such as *Interview With a Vampire* (1994, *above*).

# TERRIBLE PTEROSAURS

Novelist Arthur Conan Doyle was in no doubt about how vicious the prehistoric flying reptiles were. In *The Lost World* (a title later copied by Steven Spielberg), monsters he called pterodactyls attack a band of explorers, driving them into the trees to escape being clawed and pecked to death.

The various flying reptiles are known today as pterosaurs (*below*). Along with the dinosaurs, they developed from an early species known as archosaurs and shared air space with the first birds. The largest pterosaurs had comparatively small bodies but an enormous 12-m wingspan – the same as a small aircraft!

## FLAPPING ABOUT

There are two theories about how creatures first flew. One says they took off from the ground. The other says that by jumping out of trees for millions of years, each time parachuting down a bit further, they ended up flying!

***The Long and Short of It***
*The early pterosaurs, rhamphorhynchoids (right), all had long tails to help them fly. The first short-tailed pterosaurs, or pterodactyls (meaning "wing finger"), appeared in the Jurassic period.*

*Fish-eating pterosaurs* (below) *fall prey to a tylosaurus lurking beneath the waves.*

**Furry Flyers**
*Some pterosaurs were hairy, like bats* (below), *rather than scaly, like dinosaurs. During the Cenozoic era that followed the dinosaurs, there were also some terrifying birds, like giant diatryma* *end of the pretty* (left).

## FLAMING FOWL
No one had a bad word to say about the mythical Phoenix, except the bird itself. Every 500 years, it got fed up with life and flew to Lebanon, where it covered itself in gum. It then flew to Egypt, where it burst into flames and died. Instantly, it came to life again.

**F**LIGHTS OF FANTASY. Arthur Conan Doyle's novel *The Lost World* (1912) fed a growing interest in prehistoric animals. In a remote part of the South American jungle, time has stood still. Here, humans struggle to survive attacks by terrifying dinosaurs, "missing link" ape-people and carnivorous flying reptiles. Edgar Rice Burroughs' story, *The Land That Time Forgot* (made into a film in 1974, *below*), was a similar tale of pterosaurs surviving millions of years into the 19th century.

***Just Gliders?***
*At one time, experts believed that pterosaurs just used their wings for gliding. But most scientists now think they were good flyers that flapped their wings up and down. Hollow bones gave them a light skeleton.*

# SSSSSSNAKE!

One evening Juan Perez fell asleep in the garden of his Venezuelan home. He was woken by a sharp pain in his left leg. To his horror, an enormous boa constrictor was moving swiftly to enfold him in its coils. Aroused by his cries, neighbours arrived to find the beast slowly swallowing a crushed and lifeless corpse.

Constrictor snakes, including boas and pythons, kill their prey by squeezing it until it can't breathe, while poisonous snakes use their venom. Some snakes feed only on particular animals, such as snails and termites.

### Trust In Me
*Snakes do not literally "hypnotise" their victims before striking. The idea comes from the fact that, when faced by a swaying cobra, most creatures (including human beings!) are frozen stiff with fear.*

## HEAT-SENSITIVE ORGANS
Of the 3,000 different types of snake, about 400 are poisonous. Of these, only a few have venom powerful enough to kill a grown person. Poison is injected into the victim through a tube in the fangs (*above*). Snakes have no ears, but a sensitive feel for ground vibration. Their eyesight is fair and rattlesnakes (*right*) have a special "night eye". Two heat-sensitive pit organs on each side of the head allow the snake to detect the exact location of an animal just from its body heat.

### Fangs for the Memory
*Most poisonous snakes are vipers, with long, movable front fangs, or elapids, with short fixed fangs. A few snakes, like the African boomslang (left), have grooved fangs in the rear of the mouth. Though poisonous, they are not dangerous because they cannot inject venom quickly into large animals.*

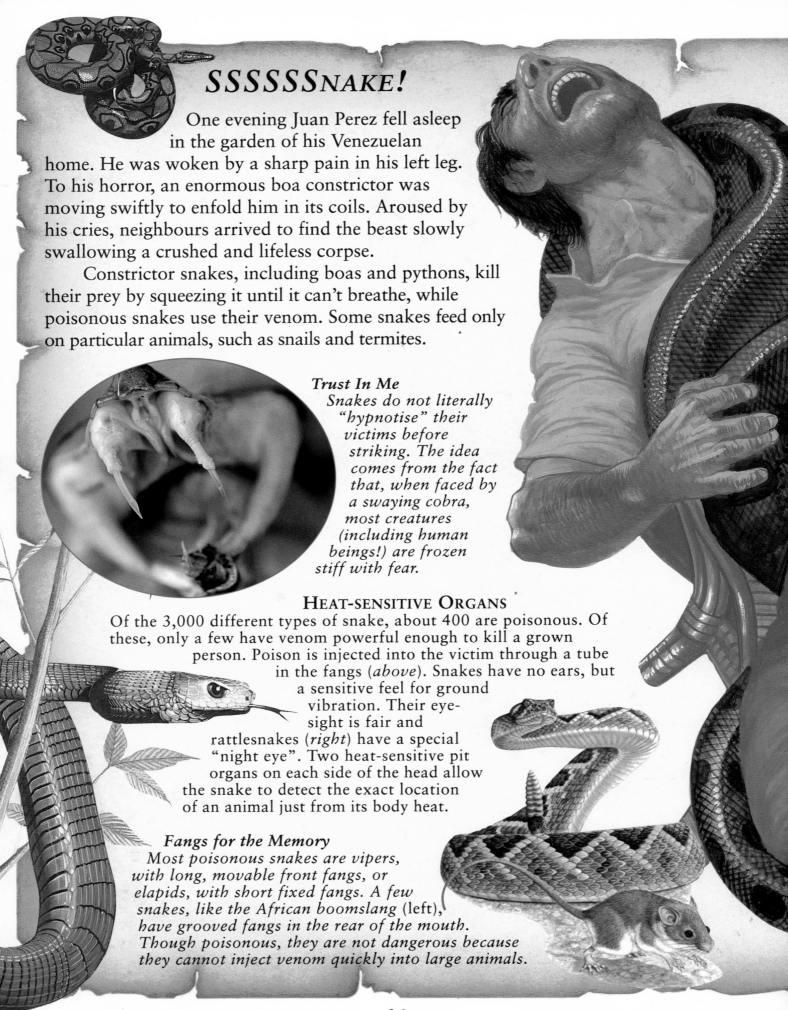

**Taking Your Breath Away**
*The huge boa constrictor, which may grow to 9 m in length, is one of the few constrictor snakes known to have killed a fully grown person* (main picture).

**S**LITHERING INTO SIN. There is something about the way a snake moves – silently squeezing and slithering – that fills most of us with repulsion. Coupled with their deadly bite, it has made them the most hated of beasts. Their image was not helped by the story of Adam and Eve. When all the world was sweet and innocent, the devil took the form of a snake and tempted Eve, the first woman, to sin. In the Greek myth of Perseus, the hideous gorgon Medusa had snakes for hair (*top*).

**The Feathery Serpent**
*The Greeks and Romans saw the snake as a guardian, while the ancient Egyptians thought the cobra represented the supreme power. To central American peoples, the feathered serpent* (left) *was a symbol of rain and crops.*

**H**YDRA-HUNTER. For his second labour, the Greek demi-god Hercules had to kill the Hydra, a multi-headed, snake-like water monster (*right*).

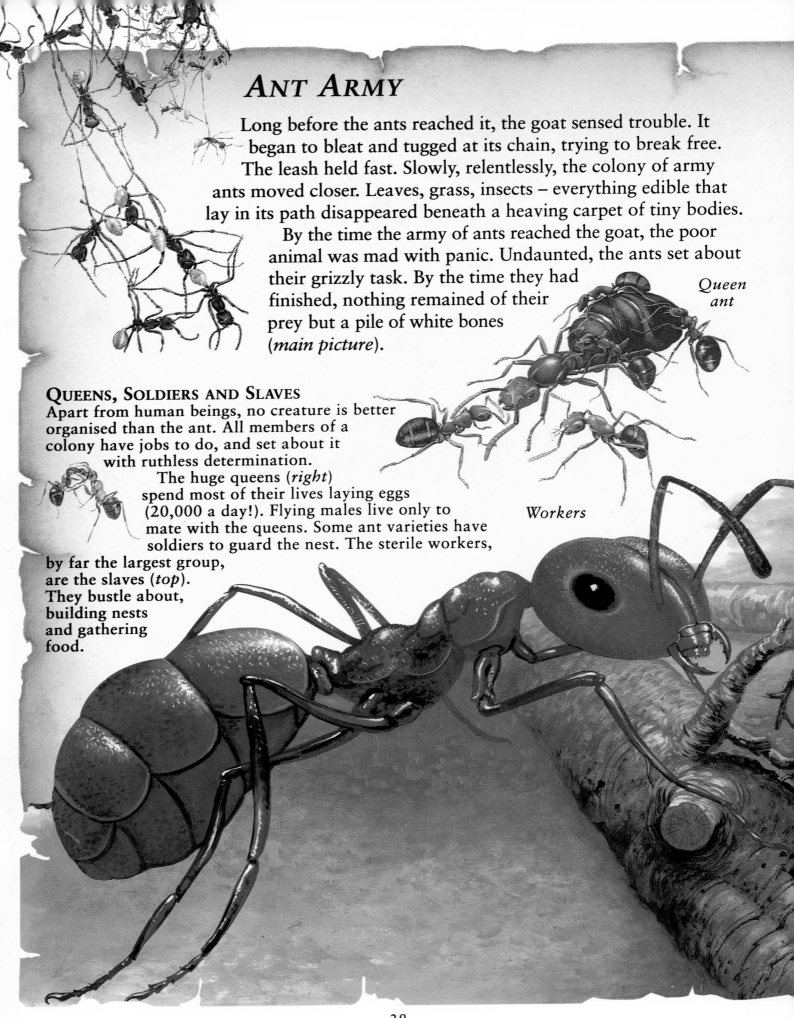

# ANT ARMY

Long before the ants reached it, the goat sensed trouble. It began to bleat and tugged at its chain, trying to break free. The leash held fast. Slowly, relentlessly, the colony of army ants moved closer. Leaves, grass, insects – everything edible that lay in its path disappeared beneath a heaving carpet of tiny bodies.

By the time the army of ants reached the goat, the poor animal was mad with panic. Undaunted, the ants set about their grizzly task. By the time they had finished, nothing remained of their prey but a pile of white bones (*main picture*).

*Queen ant*

## QUEENS, SOLDIERS AND SLAVES

Apart from human beings, no creature is better organised than the ant. All members of a colony have jobs to do, and set about it with ruthless determination.

The huge queens (*right*) spend most of their lives laying eggs (20,000 a day!). Flying males live only to mate with the queens. Some ant varieties have soldiers to guard the nest. The sterile workers, by far the largest group, are the slaves (*top*). They bustle about, building nests and gathering food.

*Workers*

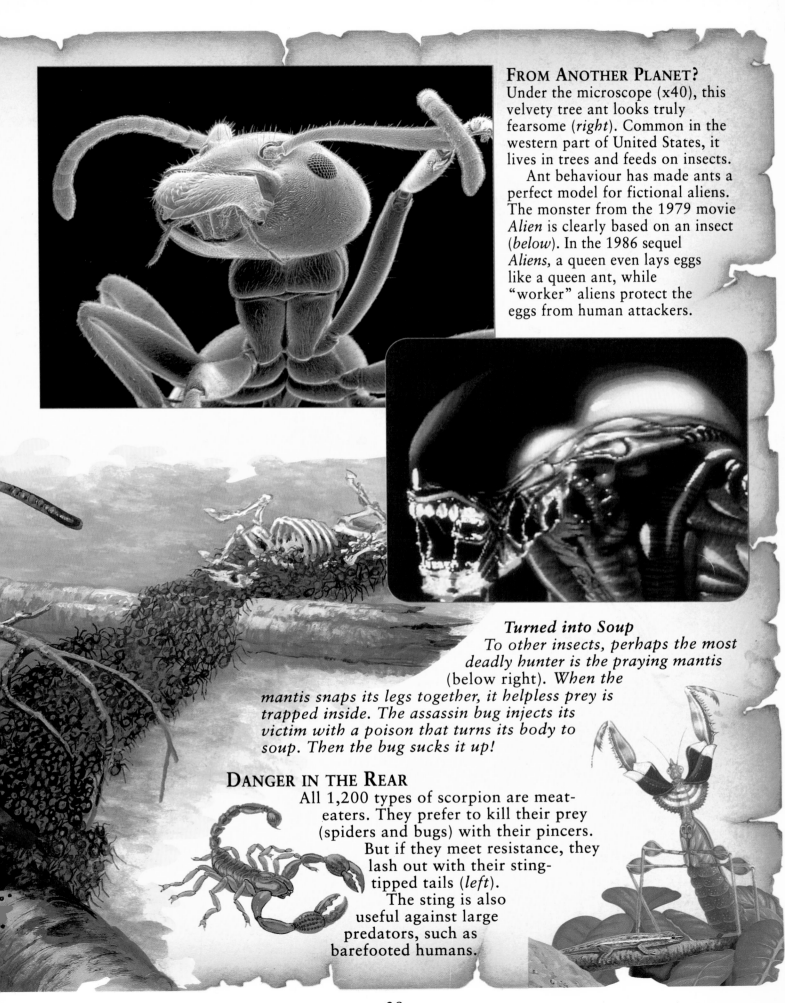

## FROM ANOTHER PLANET?

Under the microscope (x40), this velvety tree ant looks truly fearsome (*right*). Common in the western part of United States, it lives in trees and feeds on insects.

Ant behaviour has made ants a perfect model for fictional aliens. The monster from the 1979 movie *Alien* is clearly based on an insect (*below*). In the 1986 sequel *Aliens*, a queen even lays eggs like a queen ant, while "worker" aliens protect the eggs from human attackers.

### Turned into Soup

*To other insects, perhaps the most deadly hunter is the praying mantis (below right). When the mantis snaps its legs together, it helpless prey is trapped inside. The assassin bug injects its victim with a poison that turns its body to soup. Then the bug sucks it up!*

## DANGER IN THE REAR

All 1,200 types of scorpion are meat-eaters. They prefer to kill their prey (spiders and bugs) with their pincers. But if they meet resistance, they lash out with their sting-tipped tails (*left*). The sting is also useful against large predators, such as barefooted humans.

# ARACHNOPHOBIA

Few beasts are more hated than the spider. The very sight of one paralyses some people with terror – or sends them screaming from the room! Their fear is largely groundless. Of the 35,000 types of spider, only a very few are dangerous to human beings.

The hairy tarantula, for example, is a shy beast whose bite is usually less painful than a wasp sting. The bite of the larger (and hairier!) "false" tarantula (*above right*) is even less venomous. Instead of despising the humble spider, we ought to thank it for feeding on genuine pests, such as germ-carrying flies and bugs.

**Paralysed with Poison**
*Spiders have eight legs and a front end that is head and chest combined. Some of them have eight eyes!*
*Spiders grab other creatures with their chelicerae (claws), paralyse them with venom, then stores them in a silk basket until mealtime.*

## WEB SITES
Many spiders, such as the common garden spider, weave fantastic webs (*above right*) to trap their prey. Each thread is stronger than steel wire of the same thickness. Silk is made by glands in the spider's body. The silk is liquid at first but hardens into a thread when it is pulled out by little tubes called spinnerets. Spiders that live underwater spin bell-shaped webs. They fill these with air by collecting bubbles.

*Black widow*

**Danger Under the Sheets**
*A popular scene in films is the sight of a huge spider crawling towards its victim (main picture). Such films suggest that large spiders like the bird-eating spider (left) have a deadly bite. But the real killer is the tiny but deadly black widow spider.*

## Crazy Cure
*The inhabitants of medieval Italy believed the bite of the tarantula drove people crazy. The only cure for their hysteria was a wild dance (right). The mythical cure stopped being used years ago – but the dance survives as the tarantella.*

**Y**ARN SPINNING. Spiders are both good and bad in mythology. Christians reckoned it was the devil, because it trapped the innocent. The African Asanti, who had a Trickster Spider, did not think much of it either. But the ancient Egyptians, Hindus and Buddhists were more fond of it. Focusing on its amazing spinning, they linked it to creation. It was the Great Weaver, or the creature that drew the web of life out of itself. Native Americans reckoned the spider wove the first alphabet.

### The Inspirational Spider
*According to legend, King Robert the Bruce of Scotland failed six times to defeat the English. Hiding in a barn, he watched a spider trying to fix its web onto a beam (right). After seven goes, it succeeded. The lesson inspired Bruce to make one more attack. The real king won a great victory at the Bannockburn in 1314.*

### SUPER-SPIDERS
On a desert plateau near the town of Nazca, Peru, stands the world's largest pieces of art – gigantic outlines of beasts (including a 50-m spider!) between dead straight lines. As the monstrous shapes can only be properly seen from the air, it has been suggested that the ancient Nazcas (500 BC to 900 AD) must have built balloons long before anyone else!

**M**UTANT HEROES. Compared with many creatures, big-brained humans are a puny lot. But all this changes in the world of fantasy, where Spider Man (*right*) slings his web and swings from one building to another, while the super-fast Wolf Man has razor-sharp claws of steel!

# BEASTLY BUGS

The fly, one of the tiniest beasts, is also one we need to watch most closely. It feeds and breeds on rotting matter. As it does so, its mouth and legs become contaminated with germs. It then buzzes into our homes, settles on our food and even on our bodies, and so spreads infection.

But don't be too hard on the fly. It is the staple diet of many creatures. We have even found a use for the maggots that hatch out of flies' eggs. There are few better ways of cleaning up an infected wound than letting a colony of maggots chomp around in it for a while!

*Ichneumon grub*

**Grisly Grub** (above)
*The ichneumon grub hatches inside the body of a host animal, such as a caterpillar, then eats its way out.*

LORD OF THE FLIES. One name for devil, "Beelzebub", means Lord of the Flies. In the Bible's Old Testament, Beelzebub was originally the god of the Philistine city of Ekron, said to be plagued by flies. William Golding's book *Lord of the Flies* (1954) tells the story of a group of boys stranded on a desert island. They soon develop savage ways (*left*) and begin to worship a pagan god.

**The Human Fly**
*In the 1986 film* The Fly, *Dr. Seth Brundle, experimenting with transmitting matter, accidentally turns himself into half-man, half-fly when things go wrong in the laboratory (right).*

**G**OBLIN FLESH. Mythology and folklore have spawned dozens of tiny demonic beasts, from nasty little goblins to huge hairy trolls. Most people's favourite is Gollum, the hissing flesh-eater from J.R.R. Tolkien's *Hobbit* and *Lord of the Rings*.

Fairies are known as pixies in England, goblins in France, kobolds in Germany and trolls in Scandinavia.

They are all smaller than humans, but often have human features.

*locust*

### BUZZ OFF!

The clear black and yellow markings of stinging wasps (*left*), hornets and bees are nature's way of saying "Look Out"! People allergic to their venom may die after multiple stings. And when the South American "killer bees" are on the move, no one is safe. In the 1978 film *The Swarm,* a small Texas town is terrorised by a swarm of African killer bees (*top*).

### A PLAGUE ON YOU

The Bible says the prophet Moses used beastly allies to persuade the Egyptian pharaoh to release the Jews from slavery. By waving his staff, Moses brought down plagues of frogs, maggots, flies and locusts on Egypt.

Swarms of locusts (*above*) remain a curse to farmers in Africa and parts of Asia. When large groups of locusts gather, they start to travel in search of food. Swarms can contain up to 100 million insects!

# BEASTS AND BEYOND

There is no sign that our love-hate relationship with the beasts is over. We hiss them on the screen and shoot them in the wild. But we love them, too. Biologists put transmitters into anacondas to study their movements. Ecologists are even trying to re-introduce beasts into places where we have wiped them out, such as wolves into Yellowstone Park or the Scottish Highlands. Beasts, it seems, might scare us rigid, but we still can't do without them.

**Save the Beasts**
*Aware of the delicate balance that sustains life on the planet, scientists are fighting a desperate battle with poverty, greed and ignorance to preserve the few great beasts and their habitats. Most tiger species are almost gone and rhino and wild elephant herds* (top) *are under serious pressure from poachers.*

*The weird-looking weevil*

**Watch Out**
*The greatest threat to humans comes not from strange-looking beasts (like the weevil, above) but from deadly viruses too small to see with the naked eye.*

**B**EAST-MAKERS. Beware the beasts of the new millennium! In the 1950s, Russian doctors transplanted the head and front legs of a puppy onto the neck of an adult dog. The monster was hailed as a miracle. However, many films at this time warned of radioactive horrors, such as the giant ants from the 1956 film *Them! (above).*

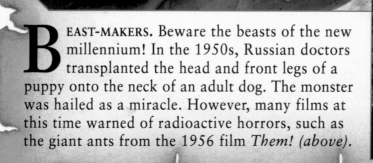

## BORN FREE

The book (1960) and film *Born Free* (1966, *left*), telling of Joy Adamson's friendship with the lioness Elsa, was one of the first signs of our changing attitude to the endangered great beasts of Africa. The Adamsons trained Elsa to hunt for food, so she would be able to fend for herself in the wild.

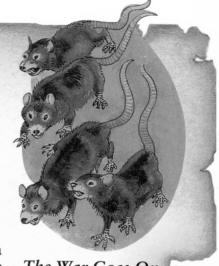

### The War Goes On

*Today's concrete jungles are by no means beast-free zones. Beside the obvious human beasts, there are rats (top) scurrying in the sewers, foxes and raccoons rummaging the garbage bins and all manner of deadly bugs, mites, flies and bacteria in every dirty nook and cranny.*

S PACE BEASTS. Just as we filled the Earth with imaginary beasts like werewolves, phoenixes and even Gremlins (*right*), so we dream of alien beasts from other worlds. But are extra-terrestrial beasts good or evil? Are they monsters, like the Martians in *Mars Attacks!* (1996), or the terrifying carnivore hiding inside people in *The Thing* (1982)? Perhaps they are gentle, like ET, or intelligent bears (*left*), like Chewbacca in *Star Wars*.

### Return of the Giants

*If the story of Steven Spielberg's* The Lost World *(page 44, left)* is to be believed, we already have the power to recreate the greatest beasts of all time – dinosaurs.

# TEN REAL BEASTS

**1 Diatryma** (*left*)
This giant bird lived about 40 million years ago. Like today's emu, it couldn't fly, but its speed and size made it a danger to the 30 cm-high ancestor of the horse, the eohippus.

**2 Krait snake**
The venom of the common krait (*Bungarus caeruleus*) is highly poisonous and makes the krait one of the most feared snakes in Asia. The krait's fangs are small so that a bite looks much like a scratch and is usually ignored for a few days while the poison starts to work. By this time it is too late for medical attention and the patient usually dies.

**3 Tiger** (*right*)
Large cats usually avoid humans, but throughout history there have been records of individual animals developing a taste for human flesh. The famous Champawat tigress was said to have killed 436 people. However, such reports are often exaggerated. Once there were 40,000 wild tigers in India – now there are just 4,000, the result of hunting, poaching and the destruction of their natural habitat.

**4 Funnel Web Spider**
The funnel web spider has a very strong poison. It often lives in Australian cities and is unafraid of humans. It strikes with great power, and can thrust its long fangs through a finger nail. Luckily, the last victims of the spider were in 1980, as there is now an antivenin (cure).

**5 Rat**
The black rat was for a long time blamed for the Black Death that killed 25 million Europeans in the 14th century. But it was the high-jumping fleas (*right*) infesting the rats' fur that really spread the plague. They carried the bacilli (germs) that caused the disease.

**6 Mosquito** (*right*)
This is truly the most dangerous of creatures to humans as infected mosquitoes spread deadly diseases, such as malaria, when they feed on our blood.

**7 Elephant**
Though elephants still kill some 200 people a year in India, compare this with the 100,000 elephants captured or killed by humans in Asia in the last 200 years.

**8 Black Bear**
The black bears of Asia kill two or three humans in Japan each year. But over 500 people have been injured by black bears worldwide in the last 30 years, mainly because they foolishly played with them because they looked so "cuddly"!

**9 Gigantosaurus** (*below right*)
This dinosaur was the largest predator that ever lived. Luckily, it lived about 100 million years ago!

**10 Humans**
Of all beasts, perhaps humans are the most destructive of all. In the last 200 years, at least 50 species of birds, 75 species of mammals and 100 other species have become extinct. Human farming, hunting and settlement have often played a major part in wiping out animals like the dodo forever. And since the first weapons were invented (*far left*), more humans have been killed by their own kind than by any beast.

# BEASTLY WORDS

**Arachnophobia** Human fear of spiders (*left*).

**Bird of Prey** A bird that lives by hunting smaller birds, reptiles and mammals like rabbits and mice.

**Carnivore** An animal that eats the flesh of other animals.

**Carrion** The dead or rotting body of an animal. Some animals, such as vultures and hyenas, live by feeding on carrion.

**Constrictor** A type of snake that kills by squeezing its prey's chest so that they cannot breathe, causing them to die.

**Dinosaur** Extinct prehistoric lizards. The word means "terrible lizard".

**Extinction** When the last living animal or plant in a species dies, the species becomes extinct. In other words, they are gone forever.

**Fangs** Teeth, usually very sharp.

**Habitat** The area in which an animal usually lives.

**Herbivore** An animal that only eats plants.

**Hibernation** When an animal passes the winter (when food is scarce) in a rested or sleeping state. It usually emerges again during spring.

**Hot-blooded** A creature that creates its own body warmth.

*The owl is a nocturnal predator*

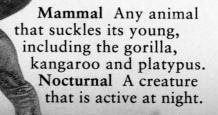

**Mammal** Any animal that suckles its young, including the gorilla, kangaroo and platypus.

**Nocturnal** A creature that is active at night.

**Omnivore** Any animal, such as a human being, that feeds on both plants and the flesh of other animals.

**Paleontology** The study of the fossilised remains of plants and animals.

**Paralysed** The loss of power or sensation in any part of the body.

**Predator** An animal that kills or preys on other animals in order to survive.

**Prehistoric animals** Beasts that lived before human records began (before about 5,000 BC).

**Prey** An animal that is hunted by a predator.

**Reptiles** Any animal that has a backbone, cold blood and scaly skin.

**Scavenger** A carnivore that picks up scraps from another animal's kill.

**Serpent** Another word for snake.

**Stalking** To hunt prey under cover of vegetation, natural obstacles or darkness in order to increase the chance of a successful capture.

**Stampede** The sudden panic-driven rush of an animal or group of animals in any direction. This is usually due to fear of an attack by a predator.

**Stealth** Moving about in a secretive manner in order to avoid being seen. Stealth can be used by the predator and the prey.

**"Were" animal** Half-human, half-animal creatures from mythology, such as the werewolf, which is part human and part wolf, and the weretiger, part human and part tiger.

# INDEX

**Photo credits** *Abbreviations: t – top, m – middle, b – bottom, l – left, r – right, c – centre.*
Cover & 27m – Paramount Pictures (courtesy Kobal); 4-5 & 15t – Universal Pictures (courtesy Kobal); 6 both, 7t, 10m, 14t, 18mr, 22, 25tl, 26t, 28t, 30 both, 32 all, 33t & 40 all – Bruce Coleman Collection; 7t, 27tc, 44ml & 45m – Warner Brothers (courtesy Kobal); 7b, 31t & 45t – Columbia Pictures (courtesy Kobal); 8 both, 10t, 12, 15m, 18ml, 24, 26m, 28b, 36 & 44b – Frank Spooner Pictures; 9t & 13b – Hutchison Library; 9m – Roger Vlitos; 11tl, 14b, 21m, 25tr, 27tr & 41t – Mary Evans Picture Library; 11m, 21b & 41b – Kobal Collection; 13t – Tri Star Pictures (courtesy Kobal); 17tm – Hammer Pictures (courtesy Kobal); 17tr & 21t – Amblin/Universal (courtesy Kobal); 19m – Hulton Getty Collection; 20 all – Fortean Picture Library; 23tr – Polygram/Universal (courtesy Kobal); 23b – Massfilm/CCC/Izard (courtesy Kobal); 26b, 39m & 43b – 20th Century Fox (courtesy Kobal); 31b – Jim Henson/ITC (courtesy Kobal); 33 – Geffen Pictures (courtesy Kobal); 35b – Amicus (courtesy Kobal); MGM (courtesy Kobal); 39t, 42m & 44mr – Science Photo Library; 42b – Castle Rock/Columbia (courtesy Kobal); 43m – Solution Pictures; 45b – Lucas Films/20th Century Fox (courtesy Kobal).